Speak To Me Lord—
I'm Listening

Speak To Me Lord— I'm Listening

Virginia Thompson

Harvest House Publishers
Eugene, Oregon 97402

SPEAK TO ME LORD—I'M LISTENING

Copyright © 1981 Harvest House Publishers
Eugene, Oregon 97402

Library of Congress Catalog Card Number: 78-55479
ISBN 0-89081-117-2

Printed in the United States of America.

Illustrated by
LIONEL KIMURA

Dedication

With love to my husband, Ernie,
and to our children, Roe, Robert
and Maaike

CONTENTS

SPEAK TO ME LORD—
I'M LISTENING

I.

At Work . . . with those whose lives I touch

CONFRONTATION

Lord, He was my professor — I was his student.
   Our acquaintance had only been slight when
   I was called into his office.
   "Did you wish to see me?" I inquired.
   "Yes, sit down please. I'll be with you in a
   moment."
I wanted to run, but I was stuck to my chair. I
   couldn't move and the atmosphere was filled
   with tension.
   "I have been assigned to be your advisor for
   your student teaching experience," he
   began. "You will make a fine teacher. I am
   sure of that even before you begin. But as a
   person I can't stand you. I cannot enter into
   an advisory capacity and feel about you the
   way I do."
All I could do was cry. What had brought this
   on?
   "When you were in my class you always
   made me feel like I couldn't teach you
   anything. You already knew it all. You are
   too perfect — too self analyzed. I have a
   desire to see you fall flat on your face."
For a solid hour he told me exactly why he
   disliked me. He had even written things
   down so that he wouldn't forget. I left his
   office in sobs of defeat because the areas
   which he attacked were the areas in which I
   felt most inadequate.

But, Lord, as I reflect back to that experience, I
    thank you for putting it into my life. I began
    at that point to look at myself as others see
    me, and to change some of my stoic
    mannerisms. You always know. You knew
    that I needed to see the truth about myself.
    Through it you have taught me to relate to
    people in a more positive way.
Thank you for caring for me. And thank you
    that today the professor is a special friend.

SCHOOL TOMORROW

Tomorrow, Lord, this school room will be filled
with children.
Some will be excited and eager.
But there will be some Danny's who feel
"Yuk" to it all.
Some will be bright and will learn in spite of
me.
Others will need special help and attention.
Each youngster will have specific and
individual needs.

I ask myself, Father, where do I fit into this
picture?
What do I have to offer?
Why am I teaching?
What are my goals?
What is it that I desire to accomplish?
What is calling from within me?

Give me the ability
to accept each child for who he is . . .
to provide fairness and understanding . . .
to help each one find their place in my
classroom.
Teach me,
to be a good listener . . .
to respect each student, and . . .
to expect their respect in return.
Don't let me use the subject matter as the
criteria for my day, but as a means to help
every student to feel good about himself.
Thank you, Lord, for the opportunity to begin
this new school year.
I look to you for wisdom and guidance.

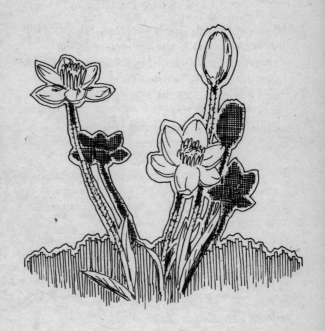

A HEART OF PRAISE

I awaken this day, God, seeking your paths for me. I prepare myself with readings and meditations from your Word. I long to know the adventure of moment by moment fellowship . . . the surety that each thought I allow to remain on the horizon of my mind is of you.

You are indeed merciful and you have assured me that although I have trials and tribulations, you have left your peace and your Holy Spirit to guide me.

I thank you with a heart bursting with praise. Fill me with you.
May the little people in my classroom see Jesus today. Please direct my thoughts, my words, and my actions that Jesus will be lifted up through my life.

It is in you, God, that I place my trust.
How excellent are your ways.

NEEDED, NOT DESERVED

Lord, what shall I do with him? This student
has been climbing the walls all day. He is a
bright fourth grader, but so immature. There
is a vast difference between what he
deserves right now and what he needs.
Grant me the ability to understand his need.
I know what he deserves and so does the rest
of the class.

"Mike, please come with me."

All eyes are on Mike now. Everyone knows that
he has pushed beyond his limits today. No
one blames me for the showdown. But
punishment is not the answer. I must
determine his basic need.

"Mike."

"Yes?"

"Mike, it's been a long day and we have
worked hard. We only have 20 minutes left
until the bell rings. Put this candy bar way
down in your pocket and see if you can make
it through the rest of the day. Okay?"

"Okay!"

Thank you, Lord, he needed that. The class is
wondering why his smile is so broad and why
he is busy with his math.

May I always be able to give to my students
what they need instead of what they deserve.

MORE THAN ANYTHING

Lord, she stands in the corner of the hallway, a sad look on her face. She is now a sixth grader. It has been two years since I was her school teacher. How can I question her without intruding? Where do I start?

"Hi Ellen."

"Hello," was her deadpan reply.

"Ellen, if you could have anything in the whole world, what would you ask for?"

"Anything?"

"Yes, anything."

"Well, I want to go horseback riding with my brother today . . . but I won't ask him. He doesn't want me along."

There is a silence now, Lord, what do I say? What prompted my first question? Please give me on-the-spot guidance.

"Mrs. Thompson," she began. "Do you mean what do I want more than anything in the whole world?"

"Yes, Ellen, that's what I mean."

"Well, what I'd really like to know is that when I die that I will go to heaven instead of . . ."

"Instead of where, Ellen?"

"Oh, you know, Mrs. Thompson."

"You can know that, Ellen."

"No, Mrs. Thompson, no one knows that for sure."

Lord, give me that ability to communicate the
depth of your love to this young one. May I
never shy away from discussing life's true
meaning with my students.
Thank you for quiet halls, moments to
question, and time to share you with others.

SOURCES OF CREATIVITY

Lord, when she asked me where I get my teaching ideas, I was tempted to accept credit for them. But I know where my ideas come from so I responded . . .

"You see I believe in the creativity of God. I believe that He has a creative solution for every problem. When I have to teach a dull lesson, I pray for a creative way to approach it. He gives me ideas. They are tailor-made for each situation."

It was then that she asked me how I developed such a strong belief in God. Thank you for providing me the opportunity of sharing my faith in your love. You are the source of all creativity. You are the Creator.

May I always be willing to give you credit. You are my God. You are my Friend. You are my Creator.

MY RESPONSIBILITY

O Father, her words caught me off guard.
 "It is apparent that you have found what the
 rest of us are looking for. I believe that you
 have a responsibility to tell us about it."
Forgive me, Lord, for being speechless. I am
 shocked to realize that this one I work with
 every day doesn't understand that she, too,
 may have peace of mind and heart. She can
 also know prayer as a way of life and may
 have you as her special friend.
I'll take her to lunch Saturday. I'll tell her.
 Defeat the fears that surround me just now,
 and give me courage to stand up and be
 counted for God and for the truth.
Let me tell her why my heart keeps singing.
 Why I sing praises to your blessed name.
 Why I sing a new song.

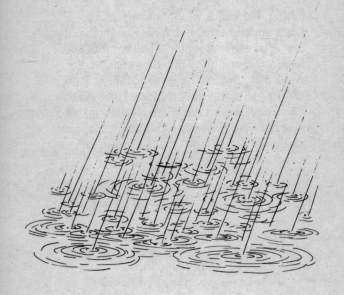

SPECIFICS

Her smile was empty, Lord. I heard echoes of
hurt behind her "Good morning."

"What about your immediate world makes
you smile today?" I asked.

"Do you mean my personal world?"

"Yes, what is it that makes you happy?"

"I can't lie," she said softly. "I'm
miserable. Tomorrow I go to court and I'm
scared."

"The divorce?"

"Yes."

God, I have not experienced what she feels
today. Give me wisdom to know how to help.

"Come with me," I told her.

I opened the supply room door and she
followed me inside. I shut the door and
locked it.

"May I pray with you?"

"Yes. I'd like that. But first you'd better
know that I get a little emotional."

"We all do—especially in times of
stress."

I reached out and took her hand.

"Father," I prayed. "Give her confidence and poise tomorrow, and give her peace throughout her day. May she have unusual strength and composure. Amen."
Through tears she said,

"Thank you. I feel better now. Your prayer was so specific and natural."

"It is like teaching," I told her. "If you have nothing specific in mind, you will not have any specific results."
Thank you, Lord, for a life of prayer.
I am grateful for the privilege of sharing you in a specific way.

NO NORMALS

Lord, what is life like for her? She does not
know what it is like to have a normal, healthy
child. Both of hers are crippled from birth.
She dresses one every day, pushes him
to school in his wheel chair, and comes at
noon to feed him his lunch. Her
determination is admirable and her love
beyond measure.

Yesterday she stopped by my classroom after
school. We talked about the day and the
prospects of the future. I had never seen her
down before. It seemed that her life was
caving in a bit.

Lord, I will always be grateful to you for the
power of prayer. When I do not really
understand, I know you do. When we
prayed, you lifted the burden. She left with a
renewed vision and greater strength.

My children run, and play, and fall in mud
   puddles. But I'm sure that she will never
   wash grass stains off of football pants. What
   is normal? Who am I to say? Normal for her
   is putting every ounce of her strength into
   helping her boys prepare for independence.
   Normal for me is children with built-in
   independence.
Thank you for no "normals." She has a job to
   do and I have a job to do. Each of us is
   unique in your sight. Each of us is equipped
   by you for our particular task.
Let me know when a little bit of my help can
   make her load lighter.

I'M EXHAUSTED

Dear Father, I am exhausted. I need your help.
My needs are immediate and urgent.
I need mental alertness to teach little people.
I need physical strength to carry out the
activities that are assigned to me.
I need emotional stability.

I believe . . .
that You will provide for me as I apply the
knowledge and promises that you have given
to me.

II.

At Home . . . with my family

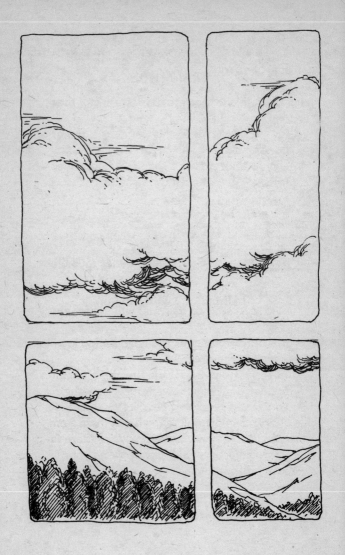

TRANSITION

Oh Lord, this is the very hardest time of the
    day.
    Please rescue me from the "before dinner
    doldrums."
        making the transition from job to home,
        listening to the children's tales,
        fighting hunger pains, and
        trying to slow down my motor
        without stopping it all together.
Hear my prayer.
    Make me sensitive to the needs of my home.
    Remove from me the cares of my job.
    May I experience joy of heart.
    May I laugh when laughter will lighten the
        tension.
    May I listen for cues of a need for my love
        and for my time.
Cheer me, God, as I look to the hills from my
    window. Let me draw strength from their
    constancy. Everyday I know that they are
    there. Even when the fog hides them from
    my view, they are there. They are there to
    show me your loving-kindness and your
    watchful care.

Lord, I praise you. You bring me rest, calm,
and comfort. You are not far from me. Even
at this moment your presence is near.
I humble my soul and my prayer is answered.
My adversity has fled from me.
I will shout for joy and be glad as I prosper
during these evening hours.

IT'S JESUS

It's Jesus who says "Come to Me."
It's Jesus who walks on the water.
It's Jesus who sleeps in the storm.
It's Jesus who calls me to rest awhile.
It's Jesus who breaks bread.
It's Jesus who heals me.
It's Jesus who controls time and space.
It's Jesus who walks my road.
It's Jesus who teaches me.
It's Jesus yesterday.
It's Jesus today.
It's Jesus tomorrow.
It's Jesus who says "Be Still . . . and Know."
It's Jesus.

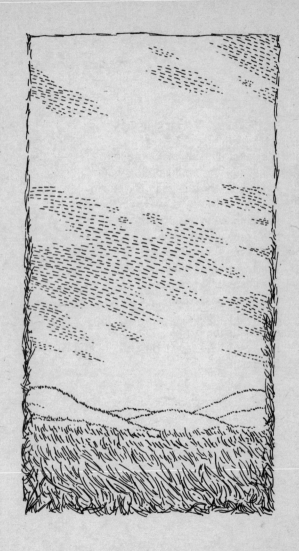

I CHOOSE

Good morning, Lord. I am happy to awaken
and to experience life today.
Today is the only day that I can be sure of
living. It's success will depend upon each
choice that I make.
I CHOOSE TO WALK THIS DAY WITH YOU.
I choose to trust my children into your
keeping.
I choose not to worry or to be anxious over
them.
I choose to meditate and to talk to you, my
special Friend. I found my way to my
Bible. Your words are soothing in my
times of pain and suffering.
I choose to refresh myself with a little
recreation. I will be childlike and carefree
while I let the breeze blow across my face
as I play a set of tennis.
I choose to accomplish something today. I
need to experience the pleasure and
satisfaction of a job well done.
I choose to spend time with a friend . . . that
we both may be renewed.
I choose to live this day one moment at a
time . . . enjoying . . . not looking back to
yesterday or ahead to tomorrow.
Thank you Lord, for the privilege of choice.

TODAY'S DEMANDS

Do not keep silent, O God. Be not still.
   My enemies have consulted together with
   one intent—to destroy me this day.
   As long as they can keep my mind boggled, I
   am helpless. Unless you come to my rescue,
   I am doomed to failure.
Every direction I turn, I look into the silent but
   glaring eyes of today's demands.
   They are too many for me to fight alone.
   Each one calls for my attention immediately.
   Not one will offer to be second.
Lord, as I wait patiently before you, impress
   upon my mind the direction that you want
   me to take.
   Focus my attention on you and cause the
   unnecessary demands to fade from my mind.
Thank you.

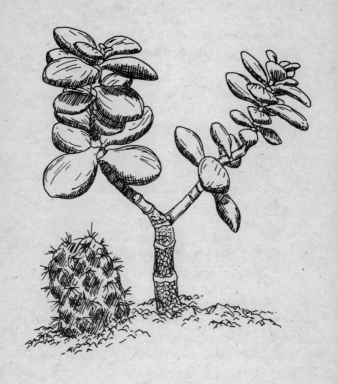

GOD'S LAWS

Do I have any other gods?
  Money? Position? Reputation?
Do I have any graven images?
  Man-made ideals?
Do I take His name in vain?
  Carelessly?
Do I reverence the Sabbath Day?
  Rest?
Do I honor my father and my mother?
  Respect? Care For?
Do I kill?
  In thought? In word?
Do I steal?
  Sneak? Deceive?
Do I bear false witness?
  Lie? Gossip?
Do I commit adultery?
  Desire? Amuse the imagination?
Do I covet?
  Against man? Against God?
"Create in me a clean heart, O God and renew
  a right spirit within me."

SELF-ACCEPTANCE

Lord,

I will never keep house like my mother.
I will never cook like his mother.
I will never have wisdom like Velda.
I will never be sweet like Dorothy.
I will never have a yard like Clydella.
I will never be organized like Nancy.
I will never entertain like Jeanie.
I will never be witty like Sue.
I will never be athletic like Marilyn.
I will never be creative like Kathy.
I will never be attractive like Molly.

I have spent 20 years trying to combine the admirable characteristics of others in order to make one perfect me.

I ask today, Lord, that you will open my eyes to the qualities that you have given to me . . . to the attributes that are uniquely mine.
May I recognize them, accept them, and thank you for them.

ONE STEP

Lord, I wait right now in your presence.
    As this day draws to a close, my mind is
    spinning.
    So many people and so many experiences
    have filled my day.
    I need calmness and I need a plan for my
    evening.
You are my guide. I do not want to run ahead of
    you.
    You have a plan—a perfect plan.
    Give me the patience to relax and wait, while
    you put your plan into operation.
Give me wisdom to determine what really must
    be done this day.
    I need discernment to separate the
    immediate needs from those that can wait.
I need discipline to lighten my load.
    I'm sure that there are some things with
    which you never intended to burden me.
Too often I try to fight all of my battles plus
    shoulder the responsibility of others, too.
    Teach me, Lord.
How wonderful it is to sit in your presence and
    to feel the peace that only you can give.
    How wonderful to have the confident
    assurance that you have been in this
    business of life a long time.
    You know how it is best lived—and you are
    near to me now, pointing out one step at a
    time.

15 MINUTE PEACE

The uncertainty of this hour is causing me to
worry, Lord.
All of the "what ifs" are crowding my mind
to the point of intolerance.
The threat of failure — of disapproval — of
criticism, all haunt me for no apparent
reason. I cannot attach a specific problem to
my frustration. But it is there nagging at me.
Teach me once more the importance of living
15 minutes at a time. I can live the next 15
minutes free from uncertainty if I so choose.
With your help, I can have peace over
anything for a short duration.
This 15 minutes I trust to you, Lord.
We will then tackle this unknown problem,
15 minutes at a time.
Thank you for teaching me the importance of
moment-by-moment peace.

WORRY

Heavenly Father,
 When I am not disciplined,
 I create worry.
 When I don't eat right,
 I worry about being fat.
 When I overspend,
 I worry about unpaid bills.
 When I neglect my housework,
 I worry unexpected company.
 When I fail to trust,
 I worry about my children.
Teach, me Lord,
 to discipline myself
 to be temperate in all things
 that I might be free from worry.

CHILDLIKE FAITH

Give me the faith of a child, Lord.
   My children don't worry about their needs.
   Their faith is simple and their trust is
   complete.
   Grant me an increased portion of faith. I
   need assurance that I did not spend selfishly
   or foolishly. I need to feel certain that my
   bills will be paid. I guess I need to know that
   you will continue to provide. You always
   have and I feel foolish to question now.
All of me and all that I possess is yours.
   And that makes me your responsibility.
   Teach me to make wise choices.
   Teach me to have faith for my needs, but to
   not clutter my life with unnecessary gadgets
   or trivial things. May I know simplicity as a
   way of life.
I thank you, heavenly Father, for your carefully
   planned instruction for my life. And I thank
   you for seeing to it that I learn my lessons
   well.
   Thank you for patiently teaching me over
   and over that you are at the controls of my
   life and that you know every detail of my
   affairs.
   You know what is best for me.
   Blessed be your Name.
   I praise you for the lessons you have taught
   me and for the lessons still to be learned.

OUR THREE GIFTS

Lord, You gave us three magnificent gifts—
    our children.
    Each is an original.
    I thank you for their uniqueness.
    I also thank you for giving us the challenge of
    trying to train them to become self-fulfilled
    adults.
    One thing, though, you didn't provide us
    with individualized sets of instructions.

About the time we arrived at a solution for dealing with our child who told lies, we found that the other two had completely different methods for deceit.

When you taught us not to become frustrated because of messy bedrooms, we learned that one of our unique little gifts was upset because we didn't notice her neatness.

When we plan a picnic, one wants hamburgers, another insists on fried chicken, while the third asks for hot dogs with catsup only.

Teach us, Lord to remember that you created all three, and that if we will remember to ask, you will provide individual guidance to us—their parents.

UNITY?

Lord God,
  Who am I?
  Where are they?
  Can we understand each other?
These three questions boggle my mind this
    hour.
  Each of us has individual desires and needs
    and each of us wants to meet the other's
    need.
  Why are we so far apart?
  Why is our understanding so limited?
My immediate need is to get away—alone.
  But in so doing I cause stress on my family.
  The oldest son is unhappy over the decision I
    made about using my car. I offered it to him
    providing he has it washed and waxed.
  He feels it is too big a price. Is it?
The young one is left to prepare dinner, to do
    the dishes, and to straighten the house.
  Outwardly, she is sweet. What are her true
    feelings?

Our middle child has been quiet lately.
He seems to be deep in thought and
somewhat disturbed. What is behind his
unusual behavior?

O God, defeat the foes that are at work against
our family unity. You have promised a song
in the night, peace in the storm, and
strength for the day. I come now to collect on
those promises.

Grant to each one of us the song of peace,
and the strength of unity.

WORSHIP

My Lord, I came to church to worship you
today.
  Give me the ability to concentrate and to
  learn to live in greater union with you.
Forgive me for my wrong attitudes.
  Forgive me for feeling hurried.
  Teach me to live a balanced life . . .
  between perfect faith and loving works.
What does the cross mean to me today?
  Was all turmoil potentially ended on the
  cross?
  Do I feel anxiety toward you this day?
  Am I experiencing anxiety or discontentment
  within myself or with another?
  Search me and show me any hurt or
  animosity that would cause me unrest and
  break our fellowship.
Deal with me realistically today.
  Reveal to me all selfishness or power
  struggles that I may be engaged in.
  Remove from me any pride or haughtiness.
Don't let me inwardly blame you, God, for my
  hurts or my failures.
  May I never feel hostile towards you.
Let me see the depth of love that the cross
  represents.
  Then I will surely know that you want only
  what is best for me.

May no barriers come between me and the
   cross.
   Let its blinding reality touch my eyes in a
   manner that will cause me permanent
   blindness to the things of the world.
   May I never again be able to see contempt
   and separation because of my spiritual pride.
As I honestly contemplate the cross this day,
   I relinquish all bitterness, all resentment,
   and all guilt.
Thank you, Lord. Truly I have been
   enlightened during my glimpse of your
   cross. Thank you for this experience in
   worship.

IT WASN'T WORTH IT

The competition was stiff for her. I saw her ten-year-old enthusiasm dwindle as the girl ahead of her put 9 out of 10 balls through the basketball hoop. It seemed that her confidence shattered as the crowd applauded her competitor.

She stepped to the free throw line, bounced the ball once, and then froze. Her toss was short. She rubbed her sweaty hands on her shorts then glanced towards the stands where I was sitting. My encouragement wasn't adequate. When her ten trys were over she walked to the bench in defeat.

Lord, I really hurt for her. But I waited. She sat quietly and watched the awards as they were presented to the winners. The crowd began to leave and I watched. She sat there alone without a backward look. I quietly called her name. She turned towards me and we met halfway down the bleachers. Her words were tearful,

"Mom, it wasn't worth your time. You drove 100 miles to see me blow it. You shouldn't have brought me."

How often I have felt the same way when I have failed. I don't want to look at you. I want to cry out that it wasn't worth it. You shouldn't have given your Son. You gave too much and I still blow it.

I am sure, Lord, that we both learned a new dimension of love that day.

Thank you for the lessons learned.

BUILDING BRIDGES

Lord God, lend me your ear and listen to this
task that the young one has asked of me.
"Mother, I need to build a bridge. It is due
in class tomorrow."
The enemy of disbelief is laughing at me
saying that I cannot help build a bridge. She
said that it can be a draw bridge or even a
suspension bridge. All around me are these
doubting darts hurling their vicious arrows
at me.
Hear me while I pray. I am seeking your
wisdom daily to keep the bridge of
communication between us.
But actually to build a bridge of wood or clay
or cardboard?
We need your help. Form in our minds a bridge
that we can build together, no matter how
simple.
Let this bridge say to her and to me that we
can always share in bridge-building.
Defeat the enemy and show your creative
power this day.
I will give all praise and glory to your Holy
Name.

THIRTEEN

I pause, Lord, in the middle of doing dishes to
   talk to you . . . about the important age
   of 13.
   I remember when my oldest son was 13. I felt
   the same frustrations that I feel today with
   my second thirteen-year-old. If I can be
   patient, he too will grow older, and then we
   can better appreciate each other.
   Today isn't the first or the last of our
   traumas. But I'll keep trying—and—God
   willing we both will learn.
   In two short years, I'll have another
   13-year-old.
   She will struggle through the fog and I,
   again, along with her.
Grant me wisdom. Double my measure of love.
   Add to my understanding.
   Let my three young people know that I really
   do care.

MOTIVATION

Lord, as I kneel beside my child's bed, I am
aware that I do not know how to motivate
him. He doesn't comprehend the need to
increase his learning power by taking time to
read. His mind is whirling with football
plays, training schedules, and dreams of
making his first million.
His goals are healthy and worthwhile, but in
order to achieve them, he needs to sharpen
his vocabulary and reading skills.
Show me how I can creatively instill in him a
desire or at least a need to take time to read.
You know what's inside of his mind and what
motivates his thinking. I pray that you will
reveal to me the secret to his motivational
mechanism.

SPEED CONTROL

It is his job, Lord, to mow their lawn. But since he is away at summer camp, we will do it for him. His sister and I. It is a big yard and neither of us have herculean strength. We will share the responsibility. May we go with happy hearts and cheerful attitudes.

I am exhausted. I went around this section three times and I'm beat. Why does she have so much more strength? Look at her—round and round she walks.

"Don't you get tired of pushing that mower?" I asked.

"No, Mom, I don't push it. It goes by itself. All I have to do is guide it and walk along behind. It is sort of like speed control. When I try to make it go faster, I just get tired because it only goes one speed."

Teach me, Lord, the lesson of "speed control" with my children.

Help me to realize that in constantly pushing them, I am only exhausting myself. If I will merely guide them and walk along with them, you will groom them into adulthood according to their individual time schedules.

And may I realize my own speed control. Help me this day to let you guide me as you walk along with me on my pathway.

ONLY ONE LIFE

Teach him, Lord, to be patient with himself.
Show him the man you are trying to create.
He wants it all right now. He isn't willing to
build brick upon brick and day upon day. He
cries for immediate, ready-made,
independence.

"I'm 18 now, Mom. I'm of age. May I live
at home—only with my own set of rules.
May I come and go as I please, and try all
of life to see what fits me?"

Wow, I wasn't ready for that. I need time.
How can I give an immediate response to
such an important question? There are so
many factors to consider. I have two younger
children to whom I am also responsible.
"I'll make a bargain with you, Son.
My decisions are based upon my 38 years
of living, and yours upon your 18 years. I
am influenced by my generation, while
you are swayed by yours. Here is what I'll
do. I'll pray 20 minutes each day about my
decision, if you will pray 20 minutes each
day about yours."
Thank you, Lord, for giving me the ability to
avoid a head-on crash until there is more
time for thought and prayer.
You always answer me when I call.

GRADUATION NIGHT

My emotions soared to an all-time high and then plunged during the past twenty-four hours.

I am left bewildered, Lord.

He walked across the stage to receive his diploma, a handsome lad with tanned skin and bleached hair. He was named ''most valuable'' for the baseball squad, and ''most inspirational'' for the basketball team.

Through my proud eyes, I saw unlimited potential.

The celebration with family and friends was exhilarating.

He favors pizza and so that's what we all enjoyed.

Congratulations came from the many happy voices wishing him well.

Then his newly acquired independence led him off to join the gang.

I could have said, ''Son, be home early.''

But I chose to let him decide.

Would his training sustain him at this time of extreme peer pressure?

Had we done our job well?

My night was sleepless. I heard every car that turned our corner. And now it is time for me to go to school.

He still isn't home.

My heart aches.

Lord, sustain me and give to me the ability to understand and to deal with my new set of problems and responsibilities as my son becomes a man.

REACH OUT

Lord, it is hard to watch a loved one flounder
and waste their life when you stand with
out-stretched arms of love to them—offering
the abundant life.
My God, my God, convict and convince them of
their waste. Reach out to them with your
love.
I will believe.
I will also release them. Release them from
my judgment.
I do believe that whatever I release on earth
will thus be released in heaven, also.

MEMORIES

Lord, I have been thinking about what I want
my family to remember when I am gone. It is
important to me that I build positive
memories.
I don't think it matters that they didn't have
a new coat this year.
I'm not concerned about how plush the
carpet is on the floor.
It isn't important for them to remember the
make of our car.
I want them to remember . . .
laughter at the dinner table,
trips to the mountains,
barbecued hamburgers and chow mein.
But most of all I want them to remember that I
taught them . . .
to be honest,
to work hard,
to love life, and
to start and end every day with a prayer.
Help me, Lord, as I attempt to build POSITIVE
MEMORIES.

ISOLATION

I have to isolate myself today, Lord.
   School has been out for two weeks and I have
   not had one minute to myself. When I drive
   to the store, someone wants to ride along.
   When I trim the shrubs, the neighbor comes
   out to chat. Even when I bake a cake, there
   are fingers in the batter. Every place I look,
   there are people — people — people.
You know that I am not a loner.
   I need people and I want people to need me.
   But today I'll come unglued if I meet one
   more person. For the next two hours, I'll
   isolate myself in this cozy little room. It is a
   cool room. It has a lock on the door. And it is
   soundproof. I'll kick off my shoes, drink this
   tall glass of tea, and enjoy my isolation.
Thank you, Lord, for the blessedness of being
   alone.

III.

At Play . . . with friends and acquaintances

GUILT-RIDDEN

Lord, I feel trouble and sorrow. I have hurt her.
I have caused her to ache. I am sorry,
Father, but the times that we have tried to be
together have been blocked. The doors have
slammed in our faces. Guilt is crowding me
today . . . guilt that cannot be dealt with
without your intervention.

You know the secrets of my heart. You know
the intents of my actions. You know the goals
that I have.

You know, God, that I have sought for your
direction at every turn. If only I had done
something so that I could say, "I'm sorry. I
love you."

But that won't work. I have not been unkind,
nor have I knowingly hurt her.

Was our friendship too dear? Was our
dependence on each other rather than on
you?

Cause her to feel close to you and be warmed
by your presence. May she look beyond my
humanness and see the beauty of your face.
May she not lose faith in you. Don't let me
be a stumbling block to her. Support her with
your arms of love and grace.

I love you, Lord, because you are always
available and ready to meet each of my daily
needs. I will call upon you for as long as I
live.

LITTLE WHITE LIES

Lord, why do I so often skirt around the truth?
Why is it easier to say "I forgot" rather than
"I didn't want to"?
Honesty is a virtue. It is also a direct command.
It is easy for me to be honest with most
people. But there are those who seem to
threaten me. I find it hard to say it like it is.
Cleanse me. Teach me new boldness.
Remove my fear of what "others" might
think of me.
Discipline me until "white lies" will not slip so
easily from my lips.
May I be honest, yes, even when I won't be
understood. May I be willing to accept
disapproval and endure momentary conflict
in order to live a life of honesty.

TO BE TRANSPARENT

Oh how I long to be transparent.
  I desire to walk along the pathway of a
  perfectly clear conscience—nothing hidden.
Search me, O God, train me and discipline me
  in your ways.
  Teach me honesty.
  Honesty with you.
  Honesty with myself.
  Honesty with my fellowman.
May I look into the eyes of everyone and be
  able to give a quiet and reverent answer for
  the HOPE that I have within me.

GUARD MY LIPS

Lord, my heart condemns me this day.
    I stated my opinions too quickly.
    Slow me down and teach me that it isn't
    always necessary to say what I think.
    You are capable of dealing with others
    without my intrusion.
    Provide me with a keen discernment as to
    when I am to keep quiet and when I am to
    speak.
Forgive me, for my injustice and for my
    judgmental attitude. Show me the road that
    you have mapped out for me, but check me
    when I expect others to follow my map.
    I desire to be patient and long-suffering with
    others.
    I pray that you will grant me a greater
    degree of your wisdom.

GRUMPY PEOPLE

Lord, I am tired of grumpy people. It is
depressing to be around those who are
unkind, impatient and dictatorial.
These are the enemies that I face today. They
won't let me be happy and express my joy.
Unlock my spirit and set me free inspite of
the enemies who would destroy my soul.
Don't let their grumpiness rub off on me.
I will continue to believe that your Spirit in me
is greater than the grumpiness which
surrounds me.

I'M SO WEAK

Lord, restore my confidence. It is hard. I am
   weak.
   Some parts of life are so much easier to
   "know" than to "live." I know the whys and
   I know the hows. But at times situations
   cause my weaknesses to stand out in bold
   letters. I feel that everyone can see my
   shortcomings and my failures.

SHE'S SO STRONG

Today it is hard, Lord. So Hard! I love her
dearly, but she is so terribly good-looking.
She has everything. Besides, she is
unshakeable. She is always constant. I do not
wish her failure, but I could be encouraged if
just once it wasn't always right with her.
Remind me that we are each unique
individuals. We each hold a special place in
your overall plan. And each of us has a gift or
talent tailor-made for us from you.

STRENGTH FOR THE DAY

Lord, it doesn't seem fair that my friend should
   be confined to her bed this day, while I am
   free to enjoy life.
   Why is it that she must suffer?
I would like to pray that she wouldn't have to
   hurt anymore. But perhaps she can never
   know you to your fullest measure if she
   doesn't walk this road of arthritic pain.

So I ask that she have strength and courage to
   live one day at a time.
Thank you for your promise of daily strength—
   enough to meet each of our needs.

BEAUTY

Lord, why do people shy away from her?
  Is it her outward beauty that causes others to
  feel that she is a cold person?
      Her style is vogue.
      Her manner is calm.
      She expresses confidence in all her
      actions.
Why is it that others don't take time to get
  acquainted with her? If they did, they too
  would see her inward beauty that I have
  come to appreciate.
      She is a good listener.
      She does not judge or criticize.
      She is generous with her time and her
      means.
      She is aware of the feelings of others.
      She laughs with them and cries with them.
She is a truly beautiful person — inside and out.
  I pray that others will be able to view the
  beautiful spirit you have given to her.

NO CLOSER, PLEASE

I don't really know her, Lord. She will only let
me get so close. She intrigues me. I want to
know her better. After I talk with her I
always feel there was more to say. Her well
of knowledge runs deep. I desire to learn
from her, but she is such an ''inside''
person.

I admire her calm, confident manner. She
seems to accept the ups and downs of life
with such matter-of-fact faith. She is truly a
beautiful person.

What lies beneath her constant manner? Are
there times of inner struggle. Is it best that
she be protected with an invisible screen?

Teach me the fine line between being available
and intruding.

May I always be available to her. But may I
never intrude when she desires to remain
''inside.''

HER HOME

Lord, I love to visit her home. It is alive with
plants and every room evidences a balance in
color and decor.
I always come away with a feeling of life and
vitality.
Perhaps it is because she has used her hands
to frame the pictures, to gold leaf the end
tables, and to macrame the wall hangings.
Most of all her home is filled with love.
She has time to sip tea and to listen to my
joys and sorrows.
She gives of herself.
She teaches me to make candles and loans
me her latest book to read.
Thank you for her home, Lord, where I am
encouraged and enriched.

A WOMAN OF WISDOM

Lord, she is truly a woman of wisdom. Thank
you for the lessons that she has taught me.
Thank you for bringing her along my road to
pick me up and minister to my needs.

"If you don't take time for the things of
God now, you won't take time later. You are
establishing patterns. In a few years they
will be set."

"You married a man who will always be
busy doing something. Accept the fact and
be grateful that he is busy with worthwhile
endeavors."

"Sometimes you will have to compromise
on the issue in order to save the child."

"They won't remember the dust on the
furniture. But they will remember your
attitude."

"Be gentle with yourself. You tend to give
yourself a 'C' grade, when you would give
someone else an 'A' for the same
accomplishment."

"Keep your antenna up at all times, and
listen carefully to His still small voice. He
will guide you."

"Be cautious. There are some people that
God has not planned for you to counsel with.
Don't become too involved."

"Carefully set your priorities. The ones
that you establish will be the ones that you
will live with."

Her words filter back through time and space
to encourage me. Thank you, God, for her
gentleness with me, and for her words of
wisdom.

A MERE MESSENGER

Lord, he is an agnostic and here I am telling
   him that you are God, that you love him, and
   you can make life worth living. He is
   listening, intently. He hasn't even touched
   the hamburger that I bought for him.
Grant me the wisdom to be able to talk his
   language.
   Don't let me mumble meaningless phrases
   and words. Give me directness and
   confidence to share you in a meaningful way.
   Also give me the willingness to leave the
   results to you. I am a mere messenger — not
Give me the willingness to leave the results to
   you. I am a mere messenger — not a Saviour.
   Plant that fact firmly in my mind. May I
   cultivate in him the seed of salvation and
   care for it through love, but then willingly
   leave the growth pattern to you.
Oh, the joy of sharing. I ate the hamburger and
   he accepted you. Thank you, Jesus.